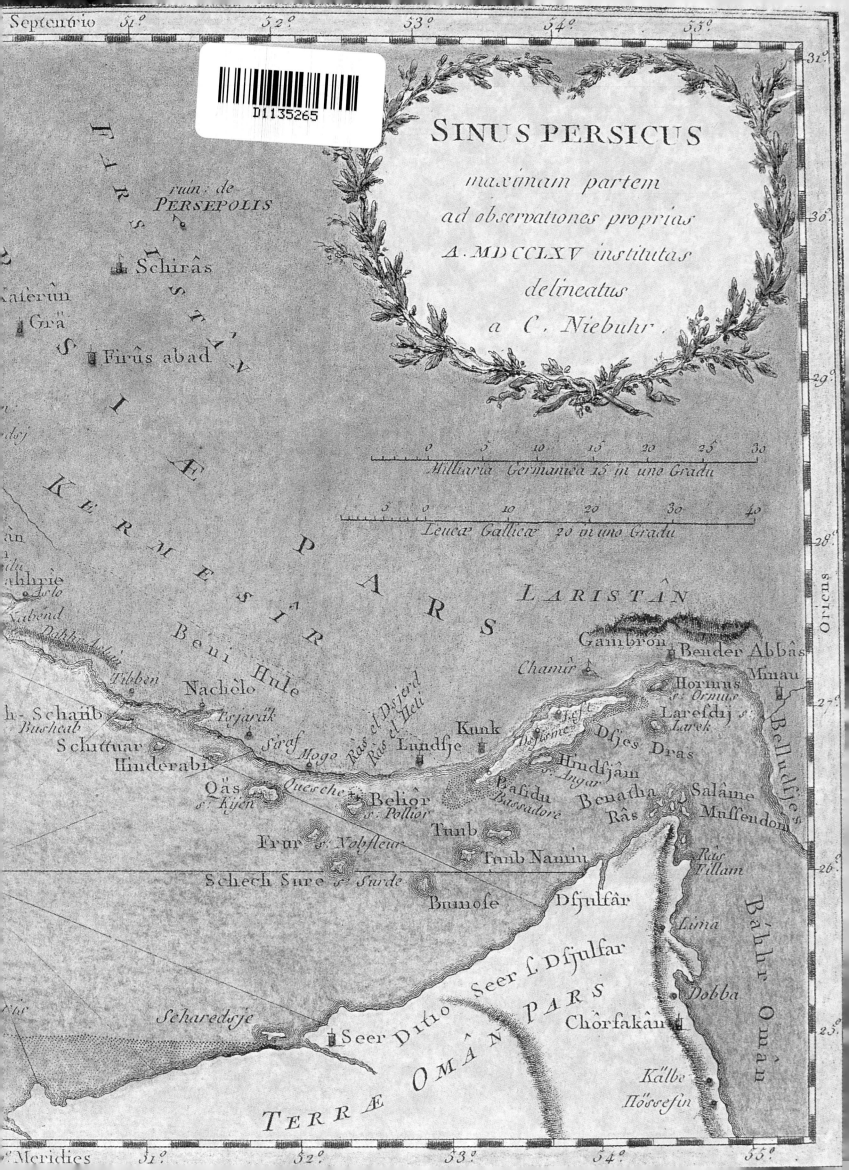

SINUS PERSICUS

maximam partem
ad observationes proprias
A. MDCCLXV institutas
delineatus
a C. Niebuhr.

Septentrio 51° 52° 53° 54° 55°

31°
30°
29°
28°
27°
26°
25°

Oriens

FARSISTAN

ruin: de PERSEPOLIS

Schirâs

Kaïerûn

Grä

Firûs abad

KERMESIR PARS

LARISTÂN

Beni Hule

Tibben

Nachelo

Dahhir Achmi

h. Schaib

Busheab

Schuttuar

Hinderabi

Oäs

s. Kjen

Tsjaräk

Siraf

Mogo

Ras el Dsjerd

Ras el Heli

Lundsje

Kunk

Quesche

Beliôr

s. Polliôr

Frur

s. Nobsleur

Tunb

Schech Sure s. Surde

Brunose

Dsjulfâr

Scharedsje

Seer Ditio Seer L. Dsjulfar

Seer

TERRÆ OMÂN PARS

Chamîr

Gambrôn

Bender Abbâs

Minau

Hormus

s. Ormus

Laresdij s.

Larek

Dsjes Dras

Hindsjâm

Angar

Dafisme

Pasidu

Bussadore

Benatha

Salâme

Râs

Mussendon

Tunb Namin

Ras Lima

Dobba

Chôrfakân

Kälbe

Nössefin

Belludsjes

Bähhr Omân

0 5 10 15 20 25 30
Milliaria Germanica 15 in uno Gradu

5 0 10 20 30 40
Leucæ Gallicæ 20 in uno Gradu

Meridies 51° 52° 53° 54° 55°

Now & Then THE EMIRATES

"A nation without a past is a nation without a present."
HH Sheikh Zayed bin Sultan Al Nahyan

Our Earth Series

Volume III

John J. Nowell *LRPS FRGS*

Foreword

Given John Nowell's well-established reputation as a photographer, with a particular interest in aerial photography, and a number of impressive books to his credit, I unhesitatingly accepted his invitation to write a foreword to this volume of photographs containing the old and the new, or more correctly, the "then" and the "now" in the United Arab Emirates. I would like to think that the British Ambassador is as well placed as anyone to see the UAE in its historical perspective. No one is in any doubt of the remarkable change that has come over the Emirates since HH Sheikh Zayed bin Sultan Al Nahyan took over as Ruler of Abu Dhabi in 1966. He and his fellow Rulers in the seven constituent Emirates have presided over a transformation as profound as seen in any country in the world.

I have been asked countless times since I returned here four years ago how I found the changes that have so altered the appearance of most of the towns and cities since the formation of the UAE in 1971. I always give the same reply: Great outward change there has been, but the most remarkable aspect of it is that the people are much the same as I remember in the 1970s.

Alongside the preservation of social and cultural values, there has been a recognition of the importance of the environment. John Nowell's book, while highlighting the changes that have occurred in the Emirates over the past sixty years, also shows how much has been preserved, how the present has grown out of the past, and how the need to bring the benefits of modern life to the Emirati people has been accomplished with great concern for the traditional pastimes and values of Emirati life and for the fragile environment of the region.

This book is a remarkable record of what has taken place in the lifetime of Sheikh Zayed. It will help the reader to understand how the UAE comes to be the Federation of Emirates that we know today.

Anthony D Harris
HM Ambassador
Abu Dhabi

Now & Then THE EMIRATES

John J. Nowell *LRPS FRGS*

Published by Zodiac Publishing, Dubai.

Zodiac Publishing, Registered Office
P.O.Box 170, Churchill Buildings
Grand Turk, Turks & Caicos Islands

Zodiac Publishing, Dubai
PO Box 35121, Dubai, UAE
Tel: 0971 4 - 2826966 Fax: 0971 4 - 2826882
e-mail: zodiacpublishing@hotmail.com

First published 1998
First reprinted 1999
Second reprint 2001

Other books in the series:

  Now & Then Abu Dhabi
  Now & Then Bahrain
  Now & Then Oman
  Now & Then Dubai

*A Day Above Oman
*A Day Above The Emirates
  A Day Above Yemen

* These books are published by Motivate Publishing

ISBN 0 9533033 0 6

British Library Cataloguing-in-Publication Data
A catalogue record for this book is available from the
British Library

Design by Nick Crawley of Zodiac Publishing
Printed by Emirates Printing Press, Dubai
"Now & Then" is a Zodiac Publishing registered trademark

Contents

UNTIL THE MAQTA BRIDGE WAS completed, the only way to cross to the main island of Abu Dhabi was to ford the channel at low tide. In 1972 a dredger completed the deep channel to make Abu Dhabi a true island. The old fort, marking and guarding the crossing point, has been restored as one of Abu Dhabi's landmarks.

Pages 8-9. AERIAL VIEW FROM HUNTER aircraft of Sharjah and old runway.

Pages 10-11. FOR THOUSANDS OF years, trade has been the international factor in the development of the Emirates. Traditional dhows could carry 200 tons of cargo but now these are dwarfed by the huge container ships such as this P & O Nedlloyd vessel, *The Jervis Bay*. Flying the flag of Great Britain, this vessel weighs almost 60,000 tons and is capable of carrying 4,038 containers.

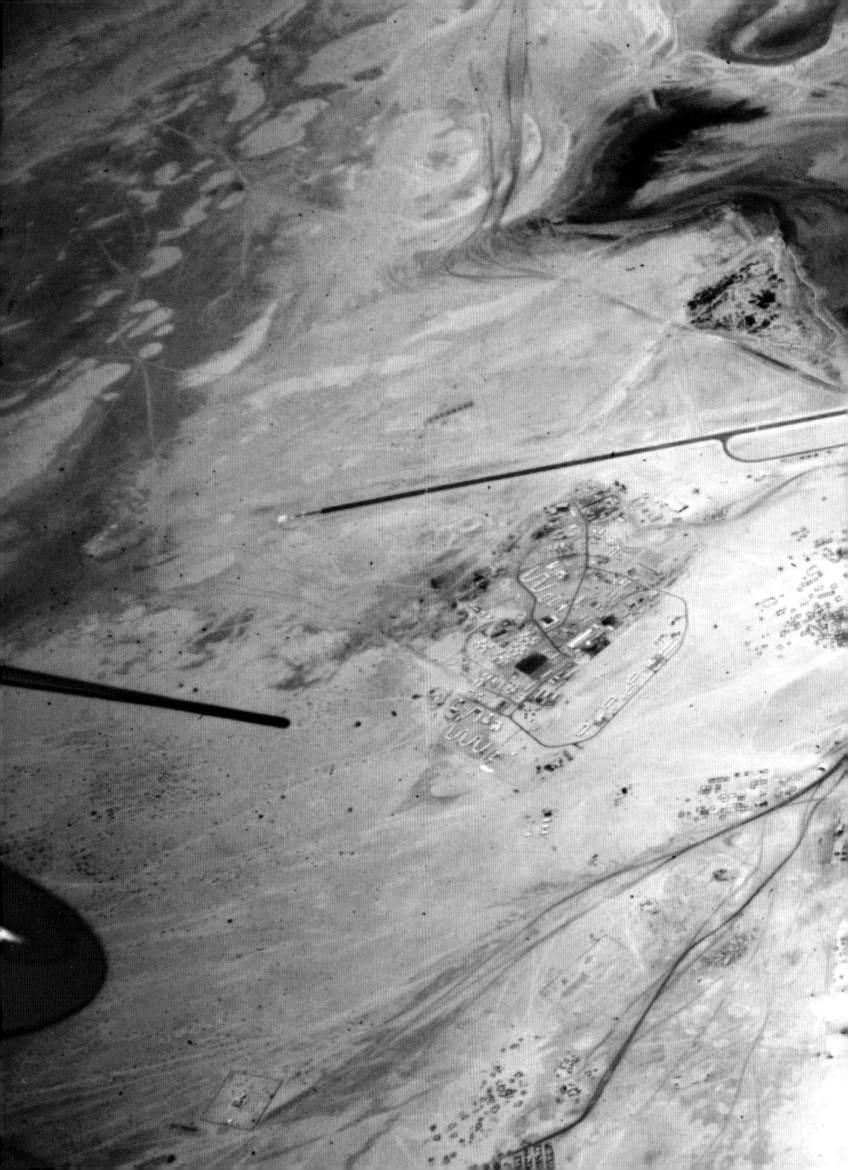

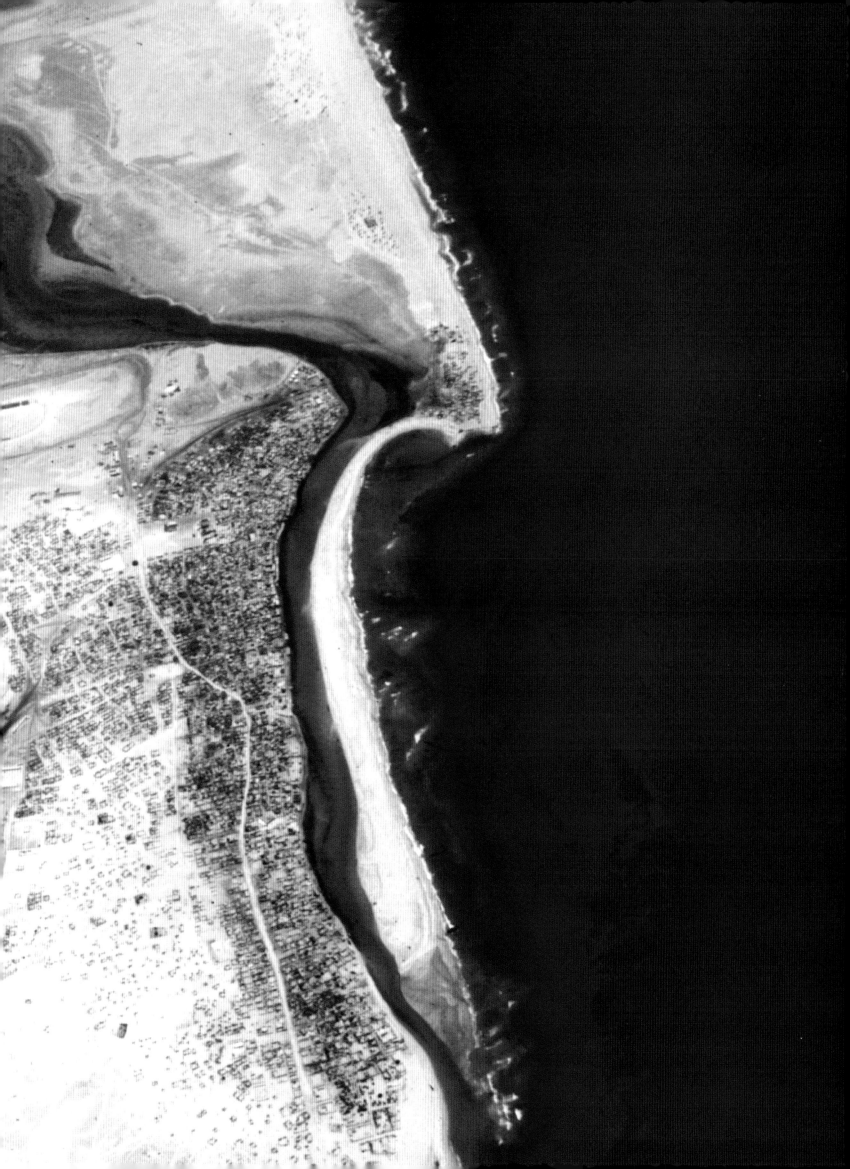

JERVIS BAY
LONDON

Introduction

A FLYING BOAT OF IMPERIAL AIRWAYS ON the River Thames. Three days later it would be in Sharjah.

Below, modern office towers overlook Dubai's Creek where traditional dhows are moored.

THE NEOLITHIC REVOLUTION TOOK PLACE IN THE MIDDLE EAST IN THE NINTH millennium BC when the inhabitants began to grow crops and domesticate animals which in turn led to the establishment of permanent settlements. These modest settlements, created around 5000 BC, were formed initially on the fertile flood plains of the Nile, the Indus and in the Tigris and Euphrates basin, and led to the development of extensive urban cultures.

With sustained sustenance, a new life style developed; that of the town-dwelling trader who recognised the need to obtain goods from other cultures. The locations of those other cultures were only generally known, but redoubtable seafarers and travellers found them and passed on directions, however rudimentary. Clay tablets may have carried instructions to help early traders find their trading partners. Thus was born the first map and the art of navigation, the catalyst that was to transform the civilisations of the world, slowly at first but, with the passing of the centuries, at an increasing pace.

By 3000 BC, the cultures of Sumer, Egypt and the Indus were well developed. They were connected and, at the same time, separated by the land bridge and seas of the Arabian Peninsula which formed a trading terminal and link between the Indian Ocean and the Mediterranean.

Historically, there was little to attract settlers in large numbers to the lands bordering the Arabian Gulf. The cruel deserts and the lack of water made it a place to be passed in transit and this led to a high degree of isolation for the area. However, both the camel caravans and the trading ships of the time needed shelter along the coast and thus the settlements of Ras Al Khaimah, Sharjah and Dubai gradually developed and prospered.

The trading dhow captains, the nakoudahs, developed a certain individuality, and their undoubted seamanship made them masters of the sea. Their skills at navigation made them famous and their written volumes, borne of the necessity to get from place to place reliably, were widely sought after. There is little doubt that charts of the Gulf were in use by the fourth century BC.

In the third century BC, the Greek scholar Eratosthenes calculated the circumference of the Earth with astonishing accuracy. He used the basic principles of geometry which still apply today. He knew of a well in Aswan, due south of Alexandria, where, at the summer solstice, the sun shone vertically downward to illuminate the bottom of the well. Eratosthenes measured the angle of the shadow cast by the sun from a pillar outside the library in Alexandria, and knowing the precise distance between Aswan and Alexandria, calculated that the circumference of the earth was 40,555 kilometres, extremely close to the actual circumference of 40,008 kilometres.

It was not until the first century AD in Alexandria that the Egyptian Claudius Ptolemy correlated all available information from ship captains and contemporary written descriptions. This he placed within the grid system which we now call latitude and longitude and produced the first scientific map of the region.

None of Ptolemy's early maps survive, many having been lost in 391 AD in the destruction of the Library at Alexandria during a Christian riot. The information contained in them, however, was preserved through the European Dark Ages by Arab universities. This knowledge re-appeared in the West during the Renaissance. Ptolemy's later maps were among the first material ever printed. Thus they played an important part in the exploration of the world by the Portuguese, Spanish and later English and Dutch navigators of the fifteenth and sixteenth centuries.

Ptolemy's sixth map, entitled "Arabia Felix" (Happy Arabia) is virtually a first century view of the Gulf. His maps influenced the founding fathers of "modern" cartography, even though they were distorted by a miscalculation of 11,200 kilometres in the circumference of the world.

Knowledge of printing developed; Abraham Ortelius printed one of the finest atlases of Ptolemy's maps in 1576, a volume of which was owned by Queen Elizabeth I. When the Arab geographer Al Idris drew his view of the world in the twelfth century, it was orientated with South at the top of the map. Today we are accustomed to seeing North at the top of the map. The map of Idris clearly showed Cyprus, the Red Sea, the Arabian Gulf and the Black Sea in a summary of known information at that time.

In the thirteenth century, the use of the magnetic compass changed the way in which navigators crossed the seas. Maps were covered with a network of criss-crossing rhumb lines that enabled navigators to leave the shoreline and cross the oceans directly. Cherubs blowing winds began to disappear from maps, to be replaced by the invaluable compass rose.

Ahmad Ibn Majid was born in Julfar in what is now the UAE in 1435. His ancestors were credited with the discovery of the magnetic compass and he developed his father's knowledge and wrote the book "First principles and Rules of Navigation." The volume, published in 1489, was used by the Portuguese until the eighteenth century. In 1498, he guided the Portuguese explorer Vasco de Gama to India and the Orient.

In 1581, Francis Drake made the first circumnavigation of the world and was knighted by Queen Elizabeth I on board the Golden Hind at Deptford on the River Thames. His feat set the tone for future English mastery of the seas.

European mapmakers, inspired by the emergence of Ptolemy's maps from the Arab universities, began a new wave of cartography supplied with information, not only from the Portuguese, such as Prince Henry the Navigator, but also from a wave of new explorers including Marco Polo. Gerardus Mercator in

OLD MAN WITH RIFLE KEEPS WATCH AS THE camels, which are his lifeline, drink at a desert water hole.

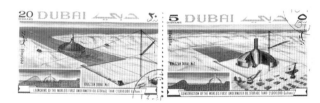

DUBAI POSTAGE STAMPS COMMEMORATE THE opening of offshore oilfields and the launch of the incredible khazzans.

HAWKER HUNTER T.7. AND AVRO Shackleton Mk II of the Royal Air Force at the Sharjah Airbase.

AN EMPIRE C. FLYING BOAT TOUCHES
down in Dubai Creek.

WORKHORSE OF THE GULF MARITIME
fleet, the venerable dhow takes on another
workhorse, a Land-Rover.

DUBAI'S THREE COMMUNITIES, CLEARLY
visible at mid-century.

1607 redrew the map of the world based on his new projection and produced the first "modern" atlas, named after the mythical Greek god who held the world on his shoulders. His copper plates, more accurate than those of Ptolemy, continued to be amended and reproduced by other Flemish cartographers such as Hondius and Bleau and in England by John Speed. Speed's atlas, published in London in 1626, contained some of the loveliest maps ever produced and are now much sought after collectors' items.

By the middle of the seventeenth century, Dutch predominance in mapmaking declined to be replaced by a new French school, led by the great French cartographer Nicholas Sanson. Encouraged by the King of France, his atlas of 1654 was not only an advance in accuracy, but also was the most elegant atlas to date. In 1690 the Sanson business was acquired by Alexis Jaillot whose descendants continued to print Sanson-inspired maps until 1780, by which time a new and more functional school of English mapmakers was emerging.

After the Napoleonic wars, cartography was revolutionised by scientific surveying, pioneered by the Royal Navy. In 1765, the invention of the chronometer, which permitted exact measures of time to be made, enabled navigators to plot their exact longitude. The Napoleonic wars had amply demonstrated the need for accurate maps if precise battles were to be fought and won.

The Ordnance Survey, the mapmaking arm of the British government used to support the army, was formed in 1791 to complement the Hydrographic Survey department of the Royal Navy. Hydrographic surveys were carried out throughout the world and became the byword for accuracy. To this day, the nautical charts are the benchmark for any seafarer; in at least one of the Emirates, the maps of the Royal Navy are now on sale, appropriately in a chandler's shop near the yard where trading dhows are still built.

The Royal Navy surveyed the coast of the Emirates in the 1830s and finally mapped its coastline: Abu Dhabi is named "Abothubbee," Qatar appears at last as a peninsula, and the "river" at Dubai disappears. In 1884, the prime meridian, an imaginary line denoting zero degrees longitude, was fixed through the small town of Greenwich on the River Thames, downstream from London. Here were also founded the Royal Observatory and the Royal Naval College where many generations of naval officers were taught the rudiments of navigation.

The First World War, from 1914 to 1918, not only involved the majority of the world's nations but also introduced both aviation and photography to the world. This merger speeded up the mapping process and gave cartographers the ability to recconnoitre ("recce") any kind of terrain, including much that was previously inaccessible. Thus deserts, mountains and remote plateaus were revealed to the airborne camera. The aerial pace of development also led to the development of radio beacons making all-weather travel possible.

After the war, the demands for travel required nations to work together in more ways than one. The first public session of the International Commission for Aerial Navigation was held on the October 25, 1922 at No 5, Old Place Yard, Westminster with Maj Gen Sir W Sefton Brancker presiding. Signatories of the 1919 International Air Convention, which governed civil aviation, included Belgium, Bolivia, France, Greece, Japan, Persia, Portugal, the Kingdom of the Serbs, Croats and Slovenes, Siam and the British Empire. The agenda covered age limits for pilots and the use of wireless apparatus. More importantly, for the benefit of international air travel, the commission laid down the first rules covering international flights over foreign territory.

In more recent times the search for oil both onshore and offshore has called for even more accurate mapping. Surveyors, geologists and seismic crews have used progressively more advanced methods of surveying to achieve the accuracy they require. The latest technique, using signals transmitted by artificial satellites, has recently been used in Abu Dhabi to confirm the work of earlier surveys.

Today, ground surveyors from companies such as MAPS of Sharjah, never go out into the field without Global Positioning System (GPS) receivers. GPS was originally developed as Star Nav by the US Navy. In the mid-1980s there were only a few satellites but now there are more than thirty. In addition, photographic mapping satellites such as the American Landsat and the French SPOT have been used for general mapping for some time though their resolution of thirty metres for Landsat and ten metres for SPOT is beginning to limit their usefulness.

In 1997, India launched a new mapping satellite which is now producing valuable data with a resolution of 5.8 metres. Such information is downloaded and used not only to produce conventional maps but also in the new science of Remote Sensing and Geographic Information Systems (GIS). Today, even telephone lines underground can be plotted.

It is a long way from Ptolemy to satellite surveying, but the Gulf, from its prehistory of trade in copper and spices to the era of oil and intercontinental jet travel has always been one of the great highways of the world. Place names may have changed since Ptolemy's time — even the name of the Gulf has changed — but for all its changes, it remains an area of great strategic importance to the world and therefore of interest to cartographers.

Cartography, aviation and photography have played their parts in the dramatic development seen across the United Arab Emirates over the last sixty years. In their time as tools of change, these disciplines by their nature are also a ready-made archive, providing valuable documentation by which future generations can catch a glimpse of the Emirates in the making, a remarkable story of a remarkable country.

MODERN DEVELOPMENT HAS TURNED Abu Dhabi into a garden city.

ELECTRICAL POWER CABLES AWAIT installation.

Chapter 1
Abu Dhabi

WHEN THE ROYAL AIR FORCE PHOTOGRAPHED ABU DHABI IN 1960, its population was estimated to be about four thousand. The old palace stood clear of the town.

THE PALACE, NOW THE CENTRE FOR DOCUMENTATION AND
Research, houses an archive of historical documents gathered
mainly from Lisbon, Goa, Bombay and London.

THE OLDEST PART OF WHAT IS KNOWN locally as the White Fort dates back to 1793. Continuous extension over the years took it to its present shape. Carefully restored, it now houses the Centre for Documentation and Research and a museum in the part of the fort that once was the Amiri Court.

WHEN THE NEW KHALIDYA PALACE
Hotel was built, it occupied a deserted
area at the extreme western end of Abu
Dhabi Island. The hotel was situated
on an isolated sand spit while dredging
work continued all around. The new
islands and land were planted with
extensive groves of palm trees to create
a lush wooded green area. Tidal action
formed new sand spits for the enjoy-
ment of both residents and tourists.

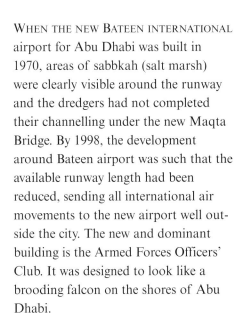

When the new Bateen international airport for Abu Dhabi was built in 1970, areas of sabbkah (salt marsh) were clearly visible around the runway and the dredgers had not completed their channelling under the new Maqta Bridge. By 1998, the development around Bateen airport was such that the available runway length had been reduced, sending all international air movements to the new airport well outside the city. The new and dominant building is the Armed Forces Officers' Club. It was designed to look like a brooding falcon on the shores of Abu Dhabi.

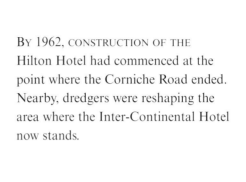

BY 1962, CONSTRUCTION OF THE Hilton Hotel had commenced at the point where the Corniche Road ended. Nearby, dredgers were reshaping the area where the Inter-Continental Hotel now stands.

OVERLEAF: SATELLITE IMAGES OVER A period of thirty years show how the city island of Abu Dhabi has developed. The main visible change has been the creation of an entirely new island to the west of the main Corniche which is now known as Lulu Island. In future years this area is to be developed extensively into a world class theme park.

RACING DHOWS CROSS THE FINISHING
line in front of the newly-built Hilton
Hotel. Only one kilometre away,
dredgers created an island which
became Bateen boat yards where
traditional and racing dhows are still
built, largely by hand, in the time-
honoured way. Traditional dhows,
workhorses of the trading fleets from
days gone by, still carry goods up and
down the Gulf coast and as far afield
as East Africa and India, ensuring that
the craft of dhow-building will
continue on Abu Dhabi island.

Chapter 2
Al Ain

JAHILI FORT WAS BUILT IN 1898 IN what was then the centre of Al Ain. Sheikh Zayed was born near this fort and spent his early years growing up here, developing his passion for hawks, hunting and horse riding. He became the ruler's representative in Al Ain in 1946. Jahili Fort became the Headquarters of the Trucial Oman Scouts in the Al Ain region. Today, the fort is surrounded by extensive gardens.

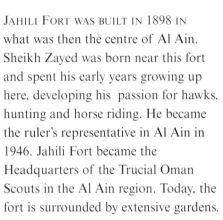

In 1960, THE HILTON AWAITED THE
first swimmers in its newly built pool.
Today, tourists are able to enjoy the
sophisticated garden which surrounds
the hotel. A new nine-hole golf course
has been created from the gravel plain
and will be extended to include a
unique water obstacle in the shape of
an adjacent wadi bed where water
flows after the sporadic rain showers.
In the background stands Jebel Hafit,
itself the site of new hotels.

LONG AGO, THE OASIS AREA WAS known as Tu'am or Al Jau and was composed of nine separate villages, six in Abu Dhabi and three in Oman. Today the area is known collectively as Al Ain, though Buraimi is within Oman. The satellite photo shows how the area has become one unit. There are no formal borders here between Oman and the UAE.

THEN, IN 1965, THERE WERE NO roads to the Liwa Oasis, a crescent-shaped series of settlements more than two hundred kilometres to the south of Al Ain. For anyone who was seriously ill, the only way to reach hospital was by aircraft. Here, a Twin Pioneer aircraft of the RAF's No 152 Squadron, approaches to land in the Liwa to carry out a Medevac mission. Today, the Liwa area has its own hospital and fine roads connect the area to the Capital.

THE TOWN OF AL AIN—THE WORDS mean "the spring"— grew up around the springs that fed several oases at the foot of Jebel Hafit. Several kilometres to the south, in the desert, an artesian well was discovered in the late 1960s at Ain Al Fayda. By 1971, development of the well had begun; it would transform this water source into the focal point of a large park. Today it is a popular resort area complete with hotel, boating canals and even a swan reserve. The area's extensive gardens and farms are spread out like a carpet below a young tourist on Jebel Hafit.

WHEN THE BRITISH ARTIST DAVID Shepherd visited the Trucial Oman Scouts (TOS) in early 1960, he was commissioned to paint the TOS Headquarters in Jahili Fort. Shepherd recalls that as he worked, an officer arrived in a swirl of dust, jumped from his Land-Rover to hurry inside, leaving the engine running and door open... essential details of TOS life which the artist captured on his canvas. Today, the fort is in the middle of Al Ain surrounded by beautiful parks.

Chapter 3
Ajman

THE NEW AJMAN KEMPINSKI HOTEL IS LOCATED ON AN
idyllic spot at the end of a long stretch of the beach at
Ajman and close to the harbour entrance. Alongside the
shores of Ajman Khor are modern ship construction and
repair facilities in contrast with the traditional dhow
building yards. Near the Diwan building is a modern
marina with the latest pleasure craft, all reflecting the
nautical heritage of the people of Ajman.

THE TRADITIONAL ACT OF ROWING
from the pearl beds has been transformed into a modern race. The
original pearling boats were built on
the shores of backwaters up and
down the Gulf, employing the tech-
niques still used today by the crafts-
men of Ajman. The keel is laid and
the ribs attached. Then, long ago,
the planks were hand-sewn together.
Now, the hand-powered bow drill is
still used to make precise holes.
Long iron nails are cast in a small
forge nearby and hammered to the
correct length before being driven
home and the heads flattened.

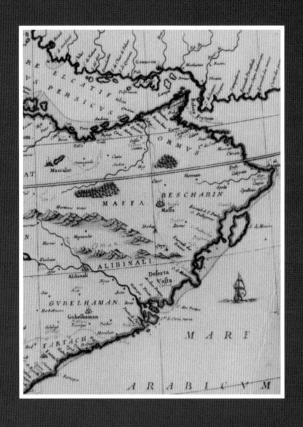

WHEN ABRAHAM ORTELIUS INCLUDED the map of the Arabian Peninsula in his new atlas in 1572, he could hardly have imagined that today, photographs are taken from circling satellites every day to show the precise geography of the peninsula. Sheikh Rashid bin Humaid Al Nuaimi, the Ruler of Ajman until 1981, surveyed his scattered domain from an armoured car. Inland, Ajman possesses three enclaves in the mountains, one adjacent to Ras Al Khaimah, one next to the Dubai enclave of Hatta and a further enclave jointly administered with Oman. Sheikh Rashid's son was able to look down on Ajman while he was a fighter pilot flying Hawker Hunters with the UAE Armed Forces.

In 1950 the fort at Ajman was the home of the ruler, Sheikh Rashid bin Humaid Al Nuaimi, who lived there from 1928 until the early 1970s, overseeing many changes in the Emirate of Ajman. Sheikh Rashid died in 1981 and was succeeded by the present ruler, Sheikh Humaid bin Rashid Al Nuaimi. The fort is now an impressive museum.

SOME ASPECTS OF DAILY LIFE IN THE
UAE never change, only the mode of
transport. Since the coming of Islam,
the devout have stopped at sunset to
face Makkah and pray. Today the
camel has given way to an ultra-
modern Land-Rover equipped with a
Global Positioning System which can
give an exact bearing and distance to
Makkah from any sand dune.

OVERLEAF — DHOWS HAVE BEEN BUILT
in Ajman for centuries. Teak was
imported from India and crafted with
amazing skill into an ocean-going
vessel which, with care, would last for a
hundred years. As the old dhow
captains, the Nakoudahs, would say to
their apprentices: "The only time you
regret having a wooden dhow soaked
in teak oil is when you're on fire."
Today, more than half of the dhows
are made of fibreglass.

Chapter 4
Dubai

THE FIRST BANK ON THE TRUCIAL COAST WAS INVITED TO SET UP IN DUBAI IN 1946 and introduced documentary credit banking procedures to replace the traditional spot cash basis of trade operations. The activities of The BritishBank of the Middle East (BritishBank) were not limited to simple commercial banking but contributed to many activities including administering the finance for the Customs Department and raising funds for the early development of Dubai, notably the key project of dredging the Creek. By 1979, the Creek had been dredged and pilings put in place. The dredged sand filled in the flood-prone areas between Shindagah and the old settlement of Dubai and made a new reclaimed area of Deira. On the reclaimed land, the new regional head office of BritishBank dominates the curve of the Creek.

WHEN THE ROYAL AIR FORCE CREWS FIRST photographed Dubai in 1930, the house of Sheikh Saeed dominated the curving sand spit called Shindagah. This area, on the extreme right of the old picture, was separated from the original settlement of Dubai by low ground which flooded at high tide before the Creek was dredged. The larger settlement of Deira forms the long spur into the bend of the Creek. Today, the three settlements are completely connected to form the nucleus of a much larger city. Sheikh Saeed's house, ancestral home of the Maktoum family, has been transformed into a museum of life in Dubai.

THE GREAT PORT OF JEBEL Ali WAS conceived by Sheikh Rashid in 1978. Local businessman Abdullah Saleh tells of sitting with Sheikh Rashid on a lonely outcrop of rock halfway between Dubai and Abu Dhabi. Sheikh Rashid, always keen to hear the opinions of others, asked Saleh what he thought of the idea of carving a port from the desert. Saleh replied that he thought many people would see the idea as ill-conceived but added that such a port would be ideal to export the aluminium from the planned smelter. Sheikh Rashid also hinted that there would be a need for a small, privately-financed hotel to cater for visitors to the port. Saleh expressed interest in the hotel. Soon after, Sheikh Rashid gave the memorable instruction: "Dig Jebel Ali Port and build your hotel."

HH Sheikh Maktoum bin Rashid Al Maktoum, Vice-President and Prime Minister of the UAE and Ruler of Dubai, pictured in 1969 while exercising his falcon in Tawi Awir. Traditional hunting has always been a favourite sport with Sheikh Maktoum. Now, the hunting falcons share the skies with another species, the British Aerospace Hawk flown by the UAE Air Force.

THEN, IN 1960, THE TRUCIAL OMAN Scouts policed the mountainous areas from bases in the Hajar Mountains. Now, the old bases have been replaced either by modern UAE army outposts or, in this case, by the luxurious Hatta Fort Hotel which retains the rifle range for recreational shooting or more traditional archery. Hatta is now a popular weekend retreat and a unique launching point for hot-air balloons.

"Dubai's offshore oil production comes from eleven reservoirs in three geological formations. To store the oil, prior to shipment, the oil was stored in huge "Khazzans", the Arabic word for storage. Each Khazzan was 90 meters in diameter and 70 meters tall. They were built by The Chicago Iron & Steel Company 20 kilometers south west of Dubai on a lonely stretch of beach that became known as "Chicago Beach". The first Khazzan was launched in 1969 with two more in 1972. Soon after a new hotel, the Chicago Beach Hotel, was built on the same stretch of beach. This was explosively demolished in 1997 to be replaced by the most luxurious resort hotel in the Middle East - The Jumeirah Beach Hotel, which was designed and construction managed by WS Atkins".

THE TINY SETTLEMENT OF DUBAI WAS first noted by the Roman chronicler, Pliny, who described the Creek and the town of Dubai as "Cynos" in the first century AD. In 1833, more than 700 members of the Al Bu Falasa tribe of the Bani Yas moved to Dubai from Abu Dhabi and formed the fledgling Sheikhdom of Dubai. In 1960, there was not a single tarmac road in Dubai. Today, the city is a magic carpet of swirling road patterns, the most elegant of which are the sweeping flyovers constructed around the Garhoud Bridge.

Chapter 5
Fujeirah

THE FORT AT FUJEIRAH WAS THE home of the ruling Al Sharqi family until the 1950s. It was also the scene of the last hostile action by British forces in the region until the Gulf War of 1990. On April 20, 1925, gunboats opened fire on the orders of the British Resident and shelled the fort for ninety minutes, killing one occupant and wounding another. The damage to the fort, which was repaired using concrete blocks, could be clearly seen until recently. Today the fort, which sits amid palm gardens on the outskirts of the modern town, is being renovated in traditional style.

BEFORE 1970, THERE WERE NO ROADS and only Land-Rovers could move freely across the rugged terrain of the northern emirates. The crescent beach at Dibba beneath the Hajar Mountains became a main thoroughfare for trade and meetings. The town of Dibba actually consists of three separate villages: Dibba Muhallab in Fujeirah, Dibba Husn in Sharjah, and Dibba Bayeh in Oman. Dibba is famous for an intense battle that took place in 633 AD. One year after the death of the Prophet (Peace Be Upon Him), three armies were sent to Dibba and a great battle ensued. Inland there is a huge cemetery, said to contain the remains of the ten thousand warriors killed in the battle. The victory by Islamic troops is traditionally considered to mark the end of all resistance to the spread of Islam throughout Arabia.

EVERY SUMMER, THE RULER OF Fujeirah and his entire court would move from the hot coastal plain into the summer palace at Al Hayl, high in the mountains, to enjoy the cool valley breezes. Today, only intrepid explorers with the right vehicle can reach these abandoned locations.

IN 1980, ZURBARAH WAS A MODEST settlement located inland from the beach and palm groves. A spur of the Hajar Mountains dipping down to the sea prevented an easy journey along the beach while affording scant protection for boats. Today, the spur has been extended into a breakwater, giving Zurbarah fishermen a useful port, while a new dual carriageway carved through the mountains links Khor Fakkan with Fujeirah.

FUJEIRAH, WHOSE DOMINANT TRIBE, the Sharqiyin, is now ruled by HH Sheikh Hamad bin Mohammed Al Sharqi, was largely isolated in bygone days. Except for coastal access, the only passage through the Hajar Mountains was along the Wadi Ham. At the highest and narrowest point, the fort at Bitna controlled the wadi. It was the central point in several battles in the eighteenth century. Twenty years ago, an intrepid driver made his way by Range-Rover to reach the fort and photographed his car with the guard. Today, Ali Numar, the same old guard, soldiers on though a modern road has bypassed the fort.

THEN, WHEN VISITING ROYAL AIR FORCE
pilots went to the Majlis, they were taken by
camel, in true Arabic style and hospitality. Now, all
travellers, visitors and residents alike, can enjoy sweeping
modern roads and the grand vistas of the East Coast.

Chapter 6
Ras Al Khaimah

A REMARKABLE PICTURE, taken in 1980, clearly shows the source of Ras Al Khaimah's agricultural tradition. Runoff from the Hajar Mountains behind the town produced the dramatic fan shape outrun of fertile land. The fan shape is also clearly visible in the modern satellite picture, skirted on two sides by green and the blue of Ras Al Khaimah's dredged lagoon.

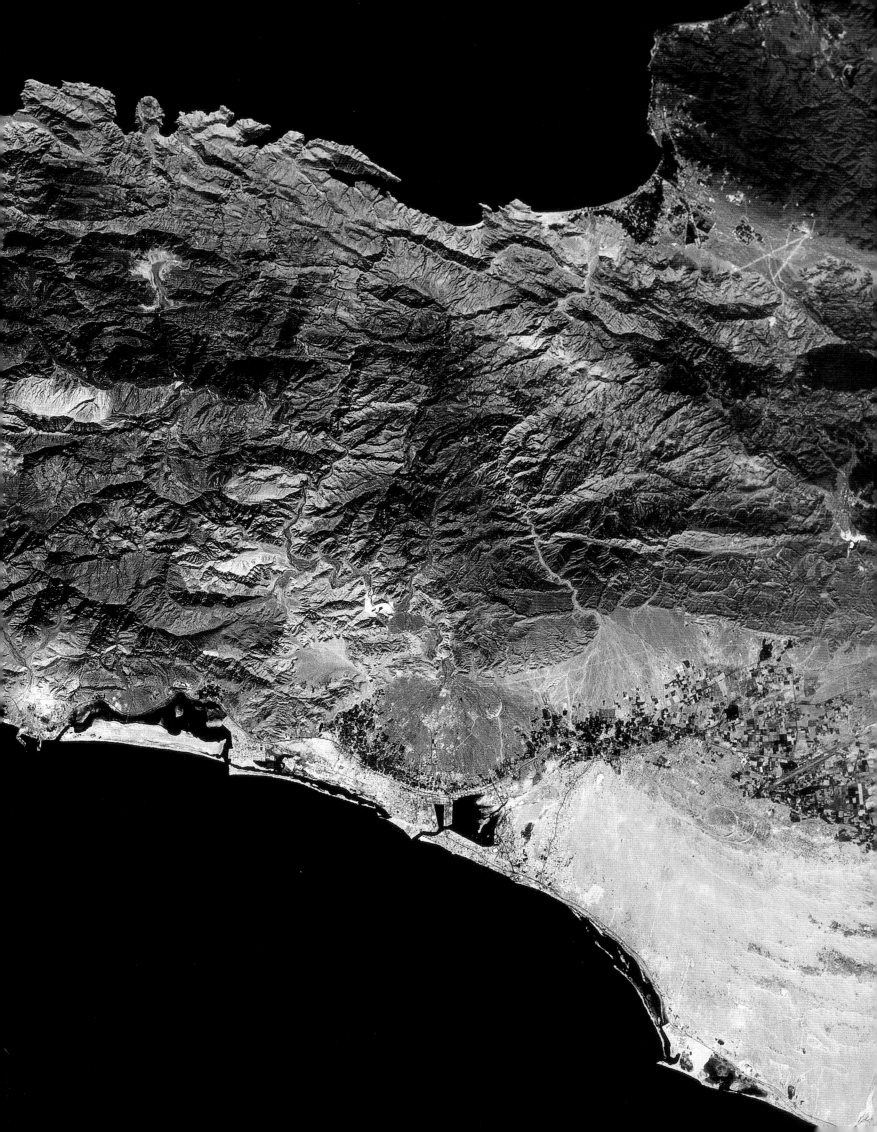

IN A FURIOUS FINALE BEFORE PEACE, BRITISH TROOPS landed to the south of Ras Al Khaimah in 1819 and breached the fort. The Qawasim defenders retreated across the Creek toward Rams and their fort at Dhayah where they eventually surrendered. After the battle the fort was destroyed and the British forces left.

IN JANUARY 1820 THE FIRST OF A SERIES OF PEACE treaties between the British and local rulers was signed at a fort at Falaya to formalise the truce — hence the name "Trucial States" by which the region was known for the next century and a half. The fighting is depicted in a full set of original lithographs on display in the Sharjah Arts Museum. These were donated by HH Dr Sheikh Sultan bin Mohammed Al Qassimi, Ruler of Sharjah.

WHEN THE MARINES OF THE BRITISH ROYAL Navy landed at the village of Rams in 1819, they dragged their cannons over five kilometres of rocky ground alternating with mangrove swamp. The Marines then bombarded the fort at Dhayah until the remaining four hundred Qawasim troops surrendered. In 1980, a Hawker Hunter took the double sequence of photographs. Today, the fort has been restored while at the thriving village of Rams, dredgers are creating land for more houses.

WHEN THE ROYAL AIR FORCE FIRST
photographed Ras Al Khaimah in 1930, they
found the largest lagoon on the western
Trucial Coast. It was here that they
negotiated with Sheikh Sultan
bin Salim Al Qasimi to estab-
lish an alighting area and
also a landing strip inland.
The proposals were met
with "significant local
opposition" but agreement
was reached. *HMS
Crocus* arrived at Ras Al
Khaimah in May 1929
and positioned fuel
onto a baraka dhow
in the khor, or
harbour.

THE MOST NORTHERLY POINT OF THE
United Arab Emirates is at the village
of Al Qir where a seven hundred metre
cliff of the Hajar Mountains meets the
sea. In 1970, this tiny village was
separated from Ash Sha'm village, just
to the south but now has expanded to
form one large settlement adjacent to
the border with Oman.

THE RAS AL KHAIMAH HOTEL WAS
built on high ground overlooking the
khor in 1971. It was some miles from
the old port. Today, dredging has
brought the sea to the hotel's doorstep
and the town has grown around and
beyond it.

OVERLEAF—THE TRADITIONAL WAY TO
reach Ras Al Khaimah was by camel
along the coast. In 1929, a new dimen-
sion to travel was added. Early that
year, surveyors from the British Air
Ministry sounded the khor of Ras Al
Khaimah and fuel was positioned by
the Royal Navy. The operations order
book of the RAF's No 203 Squadron
records that the first Supermarine
Southampton flying boat landed at
Ras Al Khaimah on May 29, 1929.

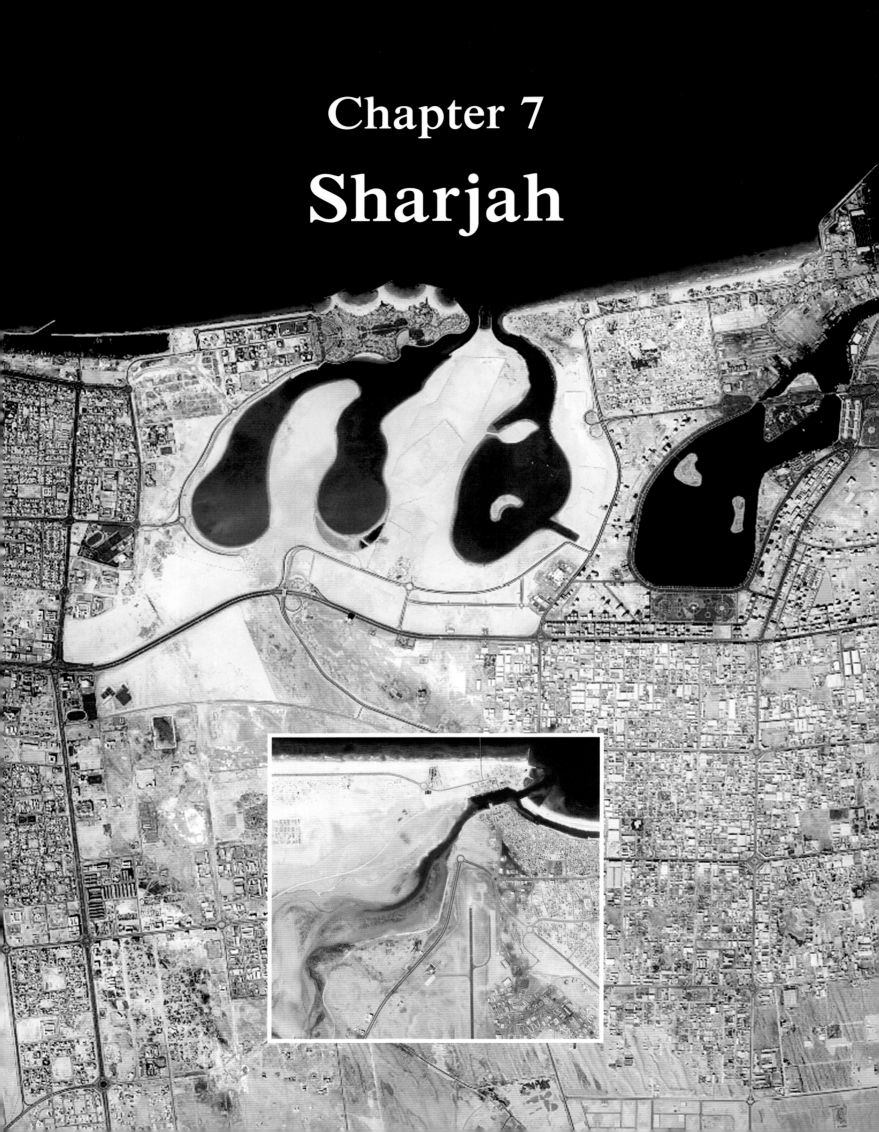

Chapter 7
Sharjah

Sharjah is the third largest of the seven Emirates and has territory on both the East and West coasts. Sharjah's place on the aviation map began in 1929 when the Royal Air Force identified a suitable area for an air strip inland from the town. An airfield opened there in 1932 as a stopover on the route to India and Australia. During the Second World War, it became a vital staging post for Allied forces. It was eventually handed over to the ruler of Sharjah in 1968. By then, the airfield was fast becoming part of downtown Sharjah. Now it has been completely absorbed by it.

THE FORT AT SHARJAH WAS BUILT TO ACCOMMODATE PASSENGERS OF IMPERIAL AIRWAYS who flew into the airfield on Handley Page HP 42 airliners. The first four passengers were flown in by Captain Horsey on October 5, 1932 on the first commercial flight to land at Sharjah. The forerunner of British Petroleum (BP) had set up operations in support of commercial aviation. To commemorate the sixty-fifth anniversary of BP's entry into the region, the renowned aviation artist Charles Thompson was commissioned to depict the event, and the original was presented to the Ruler of Sharjah, HH Dr Sheikh Sultan bin Mohammed Al Qassimi.

WHEN SHARJAH WAS PHOTOGRAPHED FROM A ROYAL NAVY
helicopter in 1965, dhows lay at the Creekside directly alongside
the old Souq Al Arsa. The unique round windtower of Bait Al
Midfa can be clearly seen and behind it is Bait Al Naboodah.
Al Hisn Fort stands in the centre of the town. Today, traditional dhows are still crowded three ranks deep alongside the quays.
The round windtower still stands in the souq and Al Hisn Fort
now forms a major junction in the centre of Boorj Avenue,
popularly known as Bank Street.

When the pilots of the RAF's No 203 Squadron first saw Khor Fakkan in 1930, it was the only sheltered anchorage on the East Coast between Muscat and the Musandam Peninsula. Now, Khor Fakkan is a bustling modern deep water terminal and regular port of call for the largest container ships travelling between the Far East, Europe and North America whose cargoes are transhipped via road or smaller feeder vessels to their final destinations elsewhere in the region.

FLYING BOATS DID LAND AT SHARJAH. THIS CANSO AIRCRAFT, A CANADIAN VERSION OF THE FAMOUS Catalina amphibian, was conducting aerial survey flights over the UAE while based at Sharjah. In the background is the old fort and control tower. Today, despite a fire in the tower, the fort has risen, like the Phoenix, from the ashes to become the thirteenth museum in Sharjah. In 1997, Sharjah was named Cultural Capital of the Arab World by UNESCO.

AL HISN FORT HAS BECOME THE
symbol of Sharjah. In the early 1950s,
camels rested in front of the Fort.
Modern development around the fort
began while the present ruler was away
at university in Cairo. "Bank Street"
started to take shape. Demolition of
the old fort began but when the ruler
heard the news, he rushed back from
Cairo to salvage the remains. Only one
tower was still standing but he found
the main doors and preserved as much
as he could. The Fort has now been
rebuilt using traditional methods and
now houses a splendid museum
covering the history of Sharjah.

DURING THE RECONNAISSANCE FLIGHTS BY THE RAF's No 203 Squadron, the survey crews photographed the Creek at Sharjah but found it too narrow to land their flying boats. However, they did find a large open space a few miles inland from the town and designated it as a suitable landing ground for aircraft with wheels. This area became Sharjah International Airfield in 1932 when the first international flight of Imperial Airways, forerunner of British Airways, landed.

Chapter 8
Umm Al Quwain

THIS PICTURE, TAKEN IN early 1930, shows the whole of Umm Al Quwain as it was then. The main settlement was on a large sand spit which was separated from the mainland at high tide. Today the area around the old village has been reclaimed and the modern city has spread all the way back to the main road.

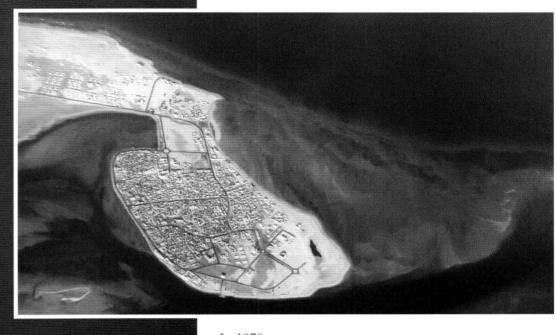

IN 1970, THIS PHOTOGRAPH ABOVE WAS
taken from a Hawker Hunter reconnaissance jet fighter. In 1998, the
colour photograph was taken from an
Antonov biplane on the descent having
dropped a number of parachutists.
Below, a satellite photograph shows the
dredged channel and how far the town
has expanded. On the promontory of
Umm Al Quwain, the Federal
Government has built the Marine and
Fish Research Centre. Inland from the
town is the largest reserve for migrant
and breeding birds in the Gulf.

THE ONLY SQUADRON OF SHORTS
Rangoon flying boats passes over
Umm Al Quwain on a reconnaissance
mission in July 1931. Only six
examples of this aircraft were built.
They were delivered in April 1931 to
No 203 Squadron of the Royal Air
Force based at Basra in Iraq. One of
the aircraft was transferred to Imperial
Airways in 1936 where it was used as a
crew trainer for the Gulf routes. Today,
squadrons of UAE microlights fly
from their own airfield at Umm Al
Quwain.

ONE PICTURE THAT SPANS THREE thousand years. Now, a modern water tower supplies the needs of Umm Al Quwain. Then, three thousand years ago, the inhabitants of Tell Abraq relied on water from the well in the centre of their settlement. The well is visible again today as a result of the work of international teams of archaeologists such as Professor Dan Potts and his team from Australia. Their findings indicate that the Gulf area has played a larger part in the development of mankind than has hitherto been supposed. At that time, the camel was first being domesticated and trade between the great civilisations was just beginning. The coastline has shifted several kilometres away to where the old fort now stands, leaving Tell Abraq high and dry.

THE WINDSOCK AT THE AIRFIELD AT UMM
Al Quwain stands on a prehistoric shell
midden, a mound of discarded snail shells
(terebralia palustris). The mound was built up
over several hundred years by the fishermen
who occupied this spot thousands of years
ago when this was the edge of the sea. Today
the water's edge lies more than a kilometre to
the west, providing sufficient space for modern flyers to take off. The Antonov aircraft
carries free-fall parachutists who perform
their precision spot landings into a nearby
water pleasure park.

WHEN A RECONNAISSANCE PARTY OF RAF PERSONNEL WAS DRIVING between the Falaj Al Moalla and the foothills of the Hajar Mountains, they were spotted by a Canberra bomber. By chance, when the pilot of the Canberra took a photograph using his aircraft mounted camera, a member of the ground party took a photograph at the same time. Today, the area now is the location of a camel race track where enthusiastic supporters urge on their favourites from a stampede of 4WDs.

Chapter 9
Acknowledgements

A Handley Page HP42 airliner of Imperial Airways is met in Sharjah by groundcrew kitted out in tropical uniform of pith helmets and shorts. To the right in the picture is one of the earliest motor vehicles to see service in the Emirates. It was used for what was then a long drive into the town of Sharjah.

THIS BOOK WAS A DISTINCT CHANGE FROM MY PREVIOUS books, *A Day Above Oman* and *A Day Above the Emirates*. For one thing, it satisfied a long-held urge to satisfy my geographic, historical and archaeological curiosity about the United Arab Emirates. With the temporary demise of CitiLink, my seaplane commuter project between Dubai and Abu Dhabi, I took a break to visit some of the military photographic archives in England which I knew to exist from my Royal Air Force days but had never had the time to explore. There I found a fascinating breed of people, new to me — the archivists who maintain immense numbers of both photographs and documents.

My first round of thanks, therefore, goes to archivists everywhere but especially to the following people:

Fred Huntley and Adrian Meredith of the British Airways archive (Pages 14 top & bottom, 56, 86 inset, 92 & 93 insets, 101, 107 and 108); Isha and Mahet of ADCO; Bill Hunt of The Ministry Of Defence photography department; Kim Hearn of the Quadrant Library of *Flight International* Magazine (Back cover); Anne Swain of the National Geographic Image Library, Washington (Page 50); Chris Morton of the Pitts River Museum, Oxford; Gordon Barclay of the British Aerospace Library at Warton (Page 61); all at the Imperial War Museum (Pages 113, 120 and 122) and the Public Records Office at Kew; Michael Gassan of the British Petroleum archives (Page 17 and 18 insets); Nabil Zakhour of ADCO; Roger Barcham and especially Andy Whithead of the Abu Dhabi Petroleum Co Ltd for access to the IPC archives (Page 16 inset) ➤

IN 1960, THE ONLY occupants of the beach at Jumeirah were occasional fisherman who kept their catch in barasti (palm frond) shelters. Today, magnificent hotels stretch into the distance along the same strip of coastline.

and the Dubai Petroleum Company (page 64 inset).

Having found the old pictures, many of them superb examples of aerial photography, I then undertook to "update" them by duplicating the photographer's vantage point wherever possible. I was fortunate to have flown with outstanding and understanding aviators of all nationalities who readily and enthusiastically Joined in the venture. They include Stu Carrie, Senior Air Traffic Controller at Ras Al Khaimah Airport; Sheikh Moh'd bin Rashid Al Mualla, determined free-fall parachutist and President of the Umm Al Quwain Flying and Parachute Sport Club, plus his fellow members; Captain Remus Ham of foot-launched self-propelled fame; Hassan Al Hamar and Malcolm Stewart; Capt. Sean Cronin, Capt. Herwig Sekotill and Capt. Hank Harrington of the Dubai Royal Flight; Major Nabil of the Dubai Air Wing; Capt. David Hopkins, Capt. Khalid Masood Butt and Capt. Moh'd Al Karnall of Fujeirah Aviation; Capt. Robert Denehy, Capt. Steve Johnson and Capt. Peter Henderson of AeroGulf, Maj Ameen Al Jenalbi and Capt. Don Sheetz of Abu Dhabi Aviation.

A very special vote of thanks goes to Sheikh Hussein Al Mualla who flew me in every emirate. With the canopy removed in his twin pusher aircraft, he clutched photocopies of the old photographs and positioned his aircraft to enable me to photograph from the same angle — an exhilarating, wind-blown and often mind-blowing experience!

Serving and retired members of the Royal Air Force played a very special part in the making of this book. It is 18 years since I left the RAF and I had almost forgotten the humour that exists throughout the force. I can happily report that the RAF's collective funny bone is alive and well.

While serving, we all battled with the "Nar Mate" tribe, a widespread collection of people who took delight in telling one that "it" — whatever "it" was — could not be done. Today, the "Nar Mate" tribe has spread and is truly international. It is therefore both reassuring that very determined people are still serving, are still doing battle with this peculiar sub-species, and that their humour is intact.➤

THE FIRST AND THE LAST FLYING BOATS TO LAND ON THE Dubai Creek were this Southampton flying boat in 1929 and the modern seaplane. The Caravan seaplane of the CitiLink service between Abu Dhabi and Dubai makes the last takeoff in 1997.

Special thanks to HE Anthony Harris, British Ambassador to the UAE, for both initiating contact with the RAF on my behalf and for kindly writing the foreword; Wg Cdr Mike Allport, the British Air Attaché in the UAE; Wg Cdr Bill Southcombe, former Air Attaché to the UAE; the late Sqn Ldr Ron Codrai, ex-No 625 Sqn and No 156 Sqn, Pathfinder Force flying Lancasters (Page 48); special thanks to Sqn Ldr Tony Cunnane for his invaluable help in setting up the Red Arrows shot and to Sqn Ldr Simon Meade — Red 1 — and all the pilots of the Red Arrows for their superb briefing and precision flying that enabled me to position exactly on the 13th floor to get just the right angle on the one and only flight pass ever to be made over the Jumeirah Beach Hotel. Special thanks to Tom Sheppard, FRGS and ARPS, former fighter pilot of No 208 Squadron, world renowned expedition leader, author, photographer and ex-Base Commander of RAF Sharjah for his generous help (Pages 8, 13, 14, 36, 79, 94, 99 and 118 insets); John Stewart-Smith, ex-No 1 (Fighter) Sqn who obviously enjoyed himself as one of the founder members — service number 200 — of the Abu Dhabi Defence Force (Pages 7, 23, 30, 33, 35, 38 inset, 47 inset, 62 inset, 68, 73, 74, 80, 84 & 85 insets, 89, 91 and 111); Kevin Dilks, ex-No 202 Sqn; and finally, my thanks to the many undocumented members of the Royal Air Force who took photographs as part of their duties in the farflung Empire and Commonwealth.

The RAF photographs are British Crown copyright, and reproduced with the permission of the Controller of Her Britannic Majesty's Stationery Office.

It was a pleasure to correspond with the artists David Shepherd OBE FRCS and Charles Thompson GAvA, ASAA, GMA, EAA who gave kind permission to reproduce their works of art. David was commissioned by the Trucial Oman Scouts to paint the TOS Headquarters at Jahili Fort in Al Ain in 1966 (Page 40) and Charles Thompson was commissioned in 1987 by British Petroleum to paint the Handley Page 42 over Sharjah Airport (Page 97).

I have enjoyed the companionship and contributions of fellow photographers Phil Blizzard of Dubai FM (Insets page 63); Moh'd Hamid Durrani (Page 1, 52 and 105); Adiseshan Shankar (IBF); Mike Cahill; Klaus Gruschwitz (Page 11); Hugh McCrae. Special thanks go to Rolf and Peter Becker and Jean-Louis Hissette of MAPS Geosystems of ➤

Sharjah for their generous access to their fascinating photographs, both old and new (Pages 25, 42, 58, 67 and 95); to Roger Le Meister (Page 4); Matt Evans and Dick Marsten of National Remote Sensing Centre in their new joint venture with the Centre of Excellence for Applied Research and Training in Abu Dhabi for the satellite images (Pages 26/27, 34 and 81); Shirley Kay; Armitage St John; Mike and Cheryl Sheppley; budding photographers Robert and William Nowell; and especially to Andrew Godber (Pages 45 inset, 60 of Sheikh Maktoum, 71, 103 and 127). In this, my first venture into self-publishing, I am grateful for the professional help from Chuck Grieve of CGA Ltd and Nick Crawley

I received a great deal of help from many officials, in particular; HH Sheikh Abdullah bin Zayed Al Nahyan and Abdul Salem Amer Lardhi of the UAE Federal Ministry of Information; HH Sheikh Sultan bin Tahnoun Al Nahyan, Khalifa Naseeb Al Amiri, Engineer Ali Saif Al Naseri and Michael Smith in AI Ain; HH Sheikh Mohammed bin Rashid Al Maktoum, Tom Merchant, Paul Wilson (Page 55) and Bron Lancaster of the Ruler's Office, Dubai; HH Sheikh Faisal bin Saqr Al Qassimi and Hisham, Al Aker of Ras Al Khaimah; Patrick Macdonald and Mike Molyneux of the Dubai Department of Tourism and Commerce Marketing; Anita Mehra and Masoud Moh'd Saleh of the Dubai Department of Civil Aviation (Page 4); Gerald Lawless, Andrew Abram and Michelle Mitschiener of the Jumeirah Beach Hotel in Dubai; Professor Dan Potts of the

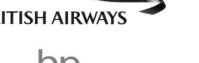

A fisherman hand-casts his net on the site where the ultra-modern Garhoud bridge now stands, complete with twisting flyovers. In the distance beyond the fisherman are the original buildings of Dubai airport as they existed in 1969.

School of Archaeology, University of Sydney; Moh'd Kunni of the Ras Al Khaimah Museum (Page 82 insets) and Jaber El Jaber of the Ajman Museum.

And finally, my thanks to the following companies whose support and encouragement made the publication of this book possible: Gerhard Hardick — the very first to put pen to cheque book — and Hagop Doghramadjian of The Hilton International Group of Hotels; David Harris of WS Atkins and Partners; Tony Northway (Page 77 inset), Matt Jones, Bruno De Bonis and Nabila Al Dahmishy of LandRover; Steve Martin, Colin Nethercote and Dina Kotby of HSBC; Walter Bailey and Bob Howard of Ducab/BICC; Nick Cochrane-Dyet, Jeremy Bowen, Graham Rose and Rick Capaccio of British Petroleum; Alan Burnett Dawn Winn of British Airways; Ken Bedwood of P & 0 Nedlloyd; Hassan Al Rostamani of Thomas Cook; Abdullah Saleh, Moh'd Gaziry, Saskia Kapinga and Debbie Kirkwood of Dutco Hotels; Kypros Tsentas and N M Naushad of UTCC Wade Adams; and finally, Jihad Hassan and Majed Al Jabr of the Crowne Plaza in Abu Dhabi.

John J. Nowell LRPS
Dubai, 1998

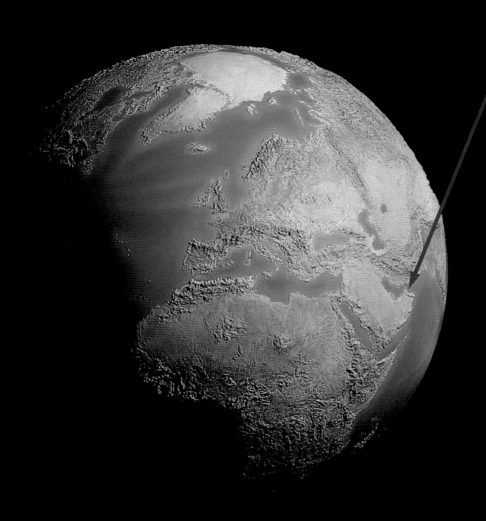

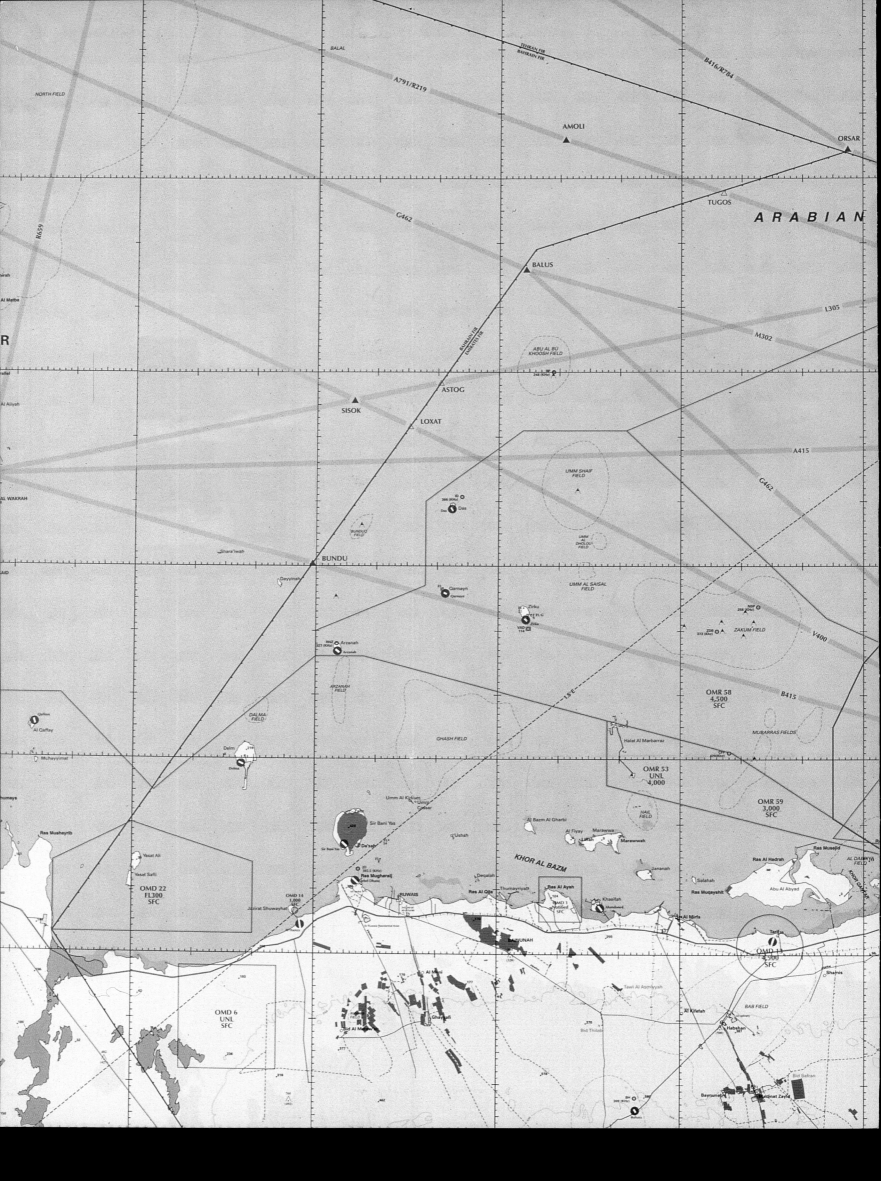